GOOD THINGS TAKE TIME
PATIENCE PENELOPE

Written By: Tawanda King-Cheek   Illustrated By: Gracy Gomel & Shakira Green

DEDICATION:

TO MY LATE MOTHER MARTHA L. KING:
Thank you for your wisdom and unconditional love.
Thank you for challenging me, and loving me, so much more than I could ever love myself.
You were the most loving and forgiving person I that I've ever met. You will always be my mother, my best friend, and my angel.
I will love you forever, and ever mom.

To my children SHAKIRA, KENNETH JR & KENDRAKIANA:
Though the journey will be tedious, always reach higher then what your eyes can see.
Be patient, hear the voice of the most
high, and allow it to order your steps.
I dedicate this book to you.

I love you past forever,
Mom

Silver

The people of Rome were not afraid to momentarily

hang fire to build an empire that would last them

many millenniums; They preferred to sweat it out in

the skin searing heat instead; Oh, what a beautiful

sight for bare eyes; To be Forbearing souls in a give

me now kind of world. So irritable, yet patiently

seeking Times desire; would that I, waiting was a

simple task for all.

~Shakira Janae Green

"Mom, I'm ready for breakfast!" yelled Penelope, as she hurried downstairs carrying her clunky school bag.

"Patience Penelope, breakfast is almost ready. Remember, you can choose something fun to do while you wait," mom said. Penelope fold her arms, "Humph," she mumbled. "Who cares about patience? I don't like patience! It's no fun being patient," she thought to herself.

Penelope wanted to make good choices, but just didn't understand why she always had to wait for something. "Is it a terrible thing if I don't like waiting?" She asked her mom. "No, sweetheart! It's not a terrible thing. Learning patience can be difficult at first, but it's something we all must learn to do, even me," her mom replied. Penelope was amazed at her mother's reply. "Even you?" She asked. "Yes, honey, there are times when I have to wait as well," Mom said with a smile. "Do you know what I do while I wait?" Her mom asked. "No mom," Penelope answered. "I think of fun things to do, and so can you." Mom said.

Penelope didn't like to wait, but doing fun things while waiting didn't sound so bad. Maybe, she could sing her favorite song like her friend Sofia when she had to wait her turn for the slide at school. Or maybe she could even help mom in the kitchen, she thought to herself.

At school, Penelope's previous ideas were long gone. It was recess, and the only thing she could think about was having a turn on the swing. The swing is her favorite, but her friend Lisa Marie got there first. "It's my turn! I want to ride the swing, please!" Penelope yelled. Lisa Marie continued swinging and said, "You have to wait your turn, Penelope!" But Penelope didn't want to wait, she didn't know how to wait, so she calls for her teacher Mrs. Churberry who was standing by the slide where Sarah and Molly were playing.

Mrs. Churberry could immediately see the frustration in Penelope's eyes. So she knelt down and gently said, "Penelope you have to be patient, and remember we take turns." Penelope face grew more intense at her teacher's reply, "I don't like waiting! I don't like patience!" she said. Suddenly, the bell rang and recess was over.

Mrs. Churberry knew Penelope didn't understand patience, so she decides to do a class project that everyone could participate in. "Okay, class! I am going to give each of you a seed to plant at home. The student who grows the seed using lots of love, and patience will win the gardening competition," said Mrs. Churberry.

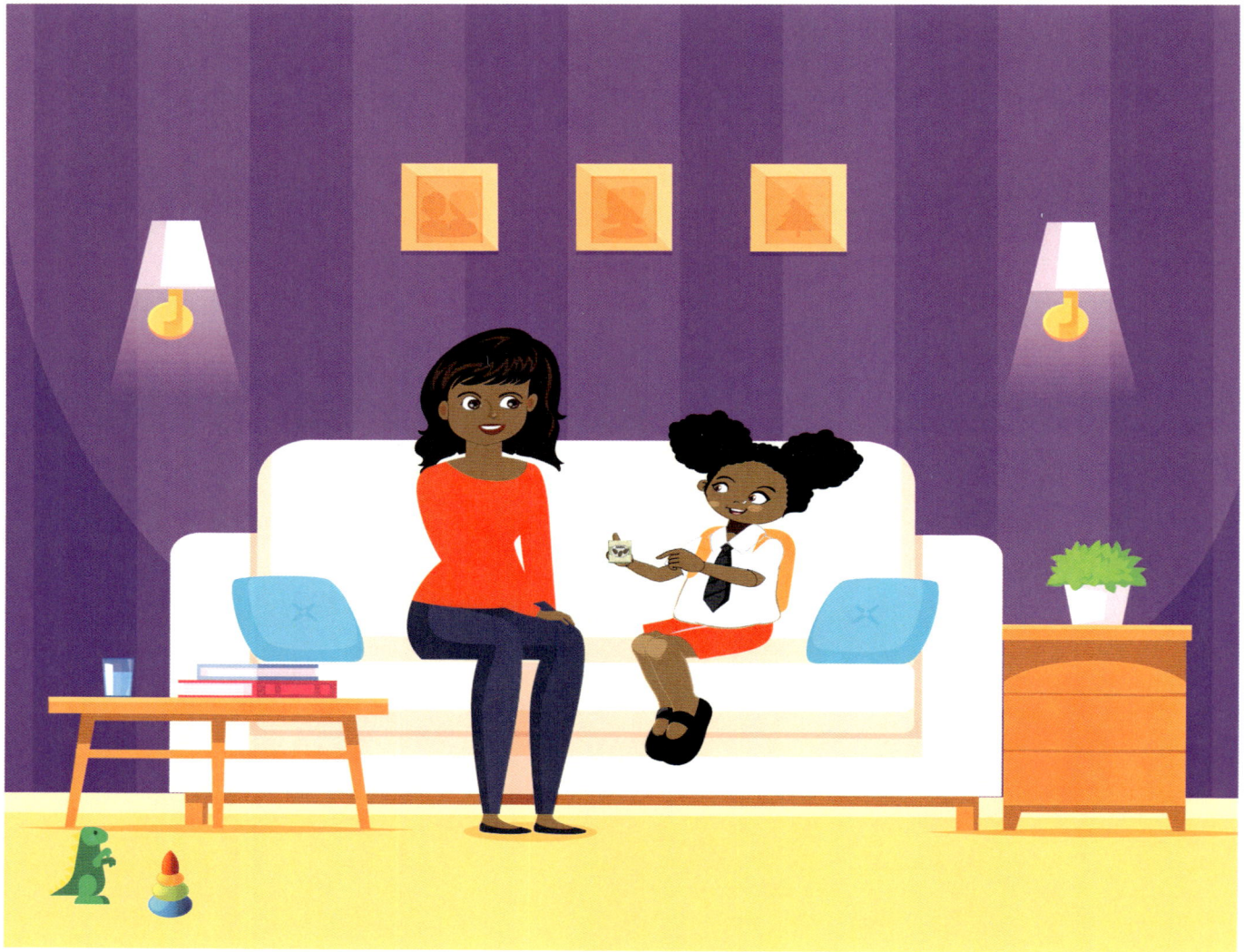

After school, Penelope takes her seed home and tells her mom all about the project. "When you plant the seed don't forget to water it, and remember you will also need patience to help it grow." Her mom said. "Patience again?" Penelope asked. "Yes, again sweetheart," mom replies with a smile.

One week had already gone by, and Penelope's seed still wasn't growing, and she began to get very impatient. "Mom why isn't my seed growing?" She asked. "Patience Penelope, good things take time, so as long as you continue to care for it using lots of love, it will grow." Her mom told her.

At school, students were also complaining that their seeds weren't growing. " I water the seed everyday and still nothing happens, it's no use," Luke said. All the other students nodded their heads in agreement. Everyone, except Penelope that is. " My mom said we should use patience, and the seed will grow." She said. Penelope had decided that this time she would use patience, and wait for her seed to grow. Her mom and Mrs. Churberry gave her the same advice and she knew they both couldn't be wrong. Finally, after two weeks Mrs. Churberry instructed students to bring back their plants.

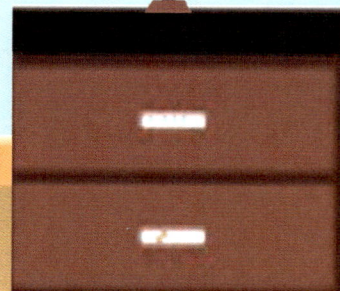

Penelope went to bed that night worried because her seed still hadn't grown. She had done everything her mom, and Mrs. Churberry told her to do. "Does patience really work? I hope my seed isn't the only one that didn't grow," she thought to herself.

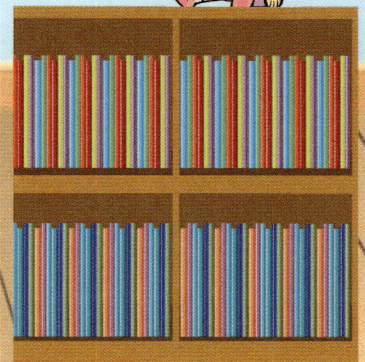

The next day, Penelope reluctantly checked her plant and was amazed by what she saw! Her seed had finally grown into a beautiful flower, and she could hardly wait to show all of her classmates.

At school, Penelope walked proudly into the classroom as everyone stared in awe, wondering how she grew the tiny seed into such a beautiful flower.

"Penelope, can you tell the class what you did to grow your seed?" asked Mrs. Churberry. "I cared for it and waited patiently for it to grow," said Penelope, smiling as she receives her gardening prize. For the first time, Penelope had finally learned that having patience could lead to something astonishing.

THE END

Review In Action:

➢ While Penelope waited for her plant to grow, she took care of it using lots of love and patience.

➢ Draw a picture describing your feelings about a time you had to wait for something. What did you do? How did it make you feel?

➢ In the story Penelope thought of fun things to do while waiting. Discuss some activities you can do while waiting at home or school.

➢ How can you help a friend or family member learn patience?

Made in the USA
Monee, IL
14 March 2021

62719821R10024